Mixed Emotions & Mood Swings

Terrance Jeffries

Presentation by *BookLeaf Publishing*

Web: www.bookleafpub.com

E-mail: info@bookleafpub.com

ISBN: 9789358366631

First edition 2023

For a muse ...past and present.

Blossom Honey

how
sweet
was
she?

well, to be honest..
she was something like
a few drops of orange
blossom honey in an
oversized mug full of
tea kind of sweet..

and right now,
i'm just waiting
for the whistle..

Through Dawn

we began as separate entities..
then through the silence of the night,
our bodies mixed, and your figure became
hidden from sinking into me..

hours passed, and we remained
an adulated brew as the light from
dawn found our tangled limbs through
a crack of never-ending drapes..

i regained a visual through illumination..
your head rested peacefully on my chest..
swooned by a heartbeat as my ribs were
comfortably cradled in your breast..
the sweet scent of your makings..
weighed heavily on my breath..

i could see,
and i could feel
just enough to know
this wouldn't end..

Rent My Bones

maybe i don't need them all..
two hundred some odd bones..
i'll dare to spare a few..
i only ask that you stay for a while and
that all of your payments come in truth..
agree to those terms, and i'll be ok
with whatever it is that you choose..

once you do..
run your hands down my rib cage
and pick from the few that are loose..
they're weakened from abuse..
be mindful if you use..
it's possible that whatever's weak in
me could be strengthened in you..

slowly, make your way around to the spine, and
please, while you pick, be kind..
there are degenerated discs that need to be fixed,
but apart from that, the structure is fine..

rent my bones..
a few i can spare..

Stiletto's Under The Mistletoe

garavani lends you a few inches..
pebbled leather and studded trim..
every penny you own is worth more than the
average, if that makes any
sense..

while lost in the means of wandering..
i found this spot and stayed..
deciding not to come any further..
no longer stressing legs, but instead watching
yours as you approached..

but for a moment, i closed my eyes..
and in doing so, i pieced together a beautiful
melody from the clattering..
and as i recognized the tempo going from fast to
sensually slow..
vigorously in rallentando..
that told me you were getting close, and when
you stopped..

you'd have no choice but to kiss me..

Mixed Toxicology

they were consumed in a crowded room..
dim-lit and exotic tunes..
twisted, tangled messes from jack
and coke mixtures..
cramped cubes meant to dilute, but
the refills were imminent..
helping them inch closer and closer
so the way that they touched was more
prevalent..

inviting publicity..
front row to sensual intensity.. there
were no masks, no cover..
just two drunken lovers..

and a gallery of affection open
for display..

Kisses In Full

i left them on you..
everywhere imaginable..
forehead kisses, they're
reassuring..
slow pecks on the neck, which
would seamlessly trickle
down your back..
then i'd gently turn you over
to lay a million on your breast..

these were the kind of lips
to never wear..
to never sleep..
to never rest..

all just to look up and see a
small depression in your flesh..

Kisses In Full: For Her

your lips..
i'll remember them
because they're full..
of love..
of pleasure..
of promise..
and they're all over..
from head to toe, they cover me..
and there are days when i wear them better than
my skin..
i've longed for this kind of affection..
because all i've known is quick pecks and
negligence..

so kiss me..

and never stop..

Envious Beings

stones filled with envy..
thrown at us from those looking in..
we were transparent and, like glass,
we shattered..
shards scattered, but we walked on
every piece..
barefoot, we bled..
leaving a trail for them to see..

WWYD

i'm not ashamed to beg and plead for it..
carefully use the right terms
whenever i have to speak for it..
go on and on and on like i prepared a speech for
it..
to really want and have a need for it..
fiend for it..
go to many extremes for it..
bare skin in any scene for it.
walk barefoot across broken glass just
to bleed for it..
leave trails for them to see how far i've come for
it..
even go to war for it..
be the last man standing if i have to compete for
it..

then be ready to serve..

even take a knee for it..

Sensory Changes

home, after slaving most of the day..
seeing the look on your face i suggested that you
should undress while i go run your bathwater..
you liked it warm, just about halfway..
i wondered what was circling your mind..
what it is you needed to say..
but you paused for a minute..
waited for me to walk away..
you sighed thinking i wouldn't hear you..
not understanding that even from a distance
we're connected..
i could feel you..

the setup..
bath bombs and rose petals..
cinnamon-scented candles placed in holders that
were gunmetal..
i remember..

you slowly got in..
soaked, while the water danced on your skin..
the warmth warranted a smile and an
explanation..
a moment of clarity..
during relaxation..

as i sat there..
all of my attention..
ready for you to vent..
then watched you lean forward
so that i could wash your back
as i listened..

Water Me

blooming..
scintillating purple petals
giving off a subtle
fragrance, and it
was pleasant..
from what i can
remember at least..

healthy and strong..
secluded, when you
hated being alone..
a loved one..
barely home and it
started to show..

as you started to go..
sweet pea..

Time Spent On Your Rose

fresh pickings and turmoil..
a sweet, but fierce presentation needed to serve a
purpose..
an eye-candy treat of delicate pinks, your
favorite color..
thought to help things simmer down before
they eventually boil over..

there's an open space on the granite countertop
where the sunbeams are direct..
but there's more shade than a sunny haze on an
island that you'll walk past and forget..

so, that's where they'll go..

stranded, left there to fend for themselves..

and it's all too familiar..

The Butterfly Effect

life turned you upside down..
spun you around as you waited for
her to bloom..
ironically, she was waiting for
you too..
giving you the time you needed
to mature..
but eager for the moment you'd
break free from your cocoon..
and when you did, she spotted you
from a distance..
making her swoon with the fluttering
of your wings..
then the uncoiling of your tongue as
you went to taste her sweet nectar..
she enjoyed the way you indulged,
but will only talk about the moment
after..

when you left her..

but maybe you'll come back
some day..

Rogue Emotions: Green

it's green..
so, i'm going..
the wheels are turning..
the rubbers burning..
i'm in a hurry to move forward..
a few thousand miles away from
our issues..
with the odometer reading the
amount of all of our miscues..
and the number keeps growing..
it's easy to track me down
because of the skid marks on the
pavement, but you shouldn't want
to..
smoke from the friction is one of
the many ways i've avoided you..

but just as i'm picking up
speed, the light turns yellow..

..maybe i should
slow down

Rogue Emotions: Yellow

or maybe i should floor it..
why break if we can't be
broken anymore..
a u-turn wouldn't turn anything
around at this point..
one foot over two pedals, i was taught
to never do that..
being half in and half out of our
situation, i told you i wouldn't do that..
but my tank's full of unleaded, and i'm headed
somewhere that's off track..
far enough to know that i'll lose time if
i decided to go back..

..and the light just turned red

..maybe i should floor it

Rogue Emotions: Red

..and so i did

mixed colors like emotions..
treated red like green because at
yellow i had a moment..
but i knew it wouldn't last..
reaching speeds on the dash i
thought i'd never come to pass..
even kept my eyes from being glued
to the rearview..
knowing if looked hard enough
there'd be a chance that i'd see you..
and i've come too far for that..
i'd be disappointed if i crashed..
disappointed if my death came from looking in
the past..
so, i mixed colors like emotions..

..and kept going

Rally

3 am circled in silence like a barrier of sorts..
company or containment, one may never know..
thoughts extracted from a crack in his skull
usually
found a home elsewhere, but this was different..

taken and given back..
taken and given back..

many of the things that left him became
felt-covered
and hollow..
served, driven back and forth until a point was
made..

unfortunately, he suffered from the self-inflicted
blunders..
errors, which made it hard for him to rest...

Addiction

you've coursed me
through constant use..

lingering..
only to settle..
letting your familiarities
come in vain..

..like abuse

grappling me..
sending euphoric waves from a brain that
contains too much for me to maintain..
pulling me outside my frame..
showing me things..
all of which i've been refusing to see…

Fire and ice

warmth exceeded its due..
time after time, provided comfort
and acted as an aide, protecting
against the elements..
the bitter cold, as you've become..
i've acquired understanding in disbelief..

..your disbelief

who would fare well in those conditions?

..your conditions

the warmth..
this way..
once was shared amongst us..
but now i circle the core alone as
you dip below dew at the surface, living
an extreme, unlike mine..

You Danced Around Us

inception, as it is..
given life from the waning moments..
the seconds leading up to something..
a decision, maybe..
one that could enable them to reach out to one
another..
to lock hands ultimately in conclusion..
the gift of beginnings..

there's a path charted for the likes of many who
wished to obtain it..
smooth yet rugged..
narrowed in spots..
and although intertwined with palms pressed..
the grip loosens as the road seemingly changes
direction..
you grow tired and malnourished of what's
sought after..
the synergy weathers because love will dance..

..and dance

..with others

Memories Sail

creased and mangled on the edges..
time has certainly done its due diligence..
our time together was quite similar as we began
to wear over the years..

i can remember the flash from when the photo
was taken and how bright it was..
being blinded by it momentarily..
nothing out of the ordinary, you flashed in all the
wrong ways..

i never felt the need to protect it because you
didn't protect us..
we were always just something for you to set
down when you didn't feel like holding on any
more..
maybe that's why something that's all of an
ounce can weigh as heavy as the burden..
so, i let go of the weight, and the photo left my
hand sailing to the pavement..

landing faced down..